BIG MAX AND THE OIL R

Fred came home from school.
"Hello, Big Max."
"Be quiet. I'm trying to watch the news,"
said Big Max.

1

"What has happened?" asked Fred.

"An oil rig is in danger.
The weather is very bad.
It is too dangerous for anyone to go there.
But a robot could save the oil rig,"
said Big Max.

"We have to go and save the oil rig," said Big Max.

"It's too dangerous," said Fred.
"Too bad," said Big Max. "I need your help."

Fred and Big Max flew out of the window.
"Hold tight," said the robot.
"Don't let the wind blow you away."

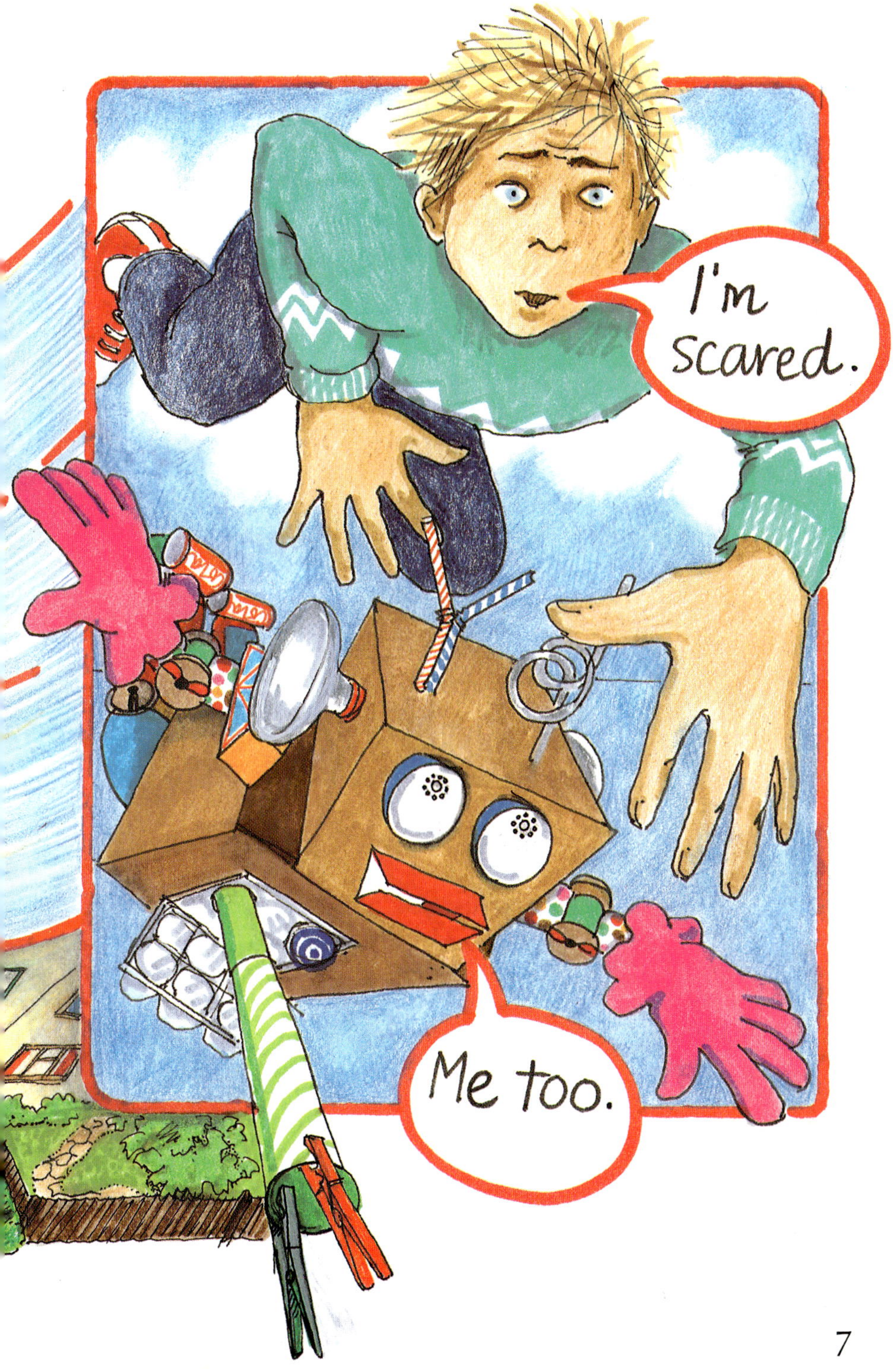
I'm scared.
Me too.

They found the oil rig.
The men on the oil rig looked scared.

The wind was blowing very hard.
The waves were very big.
"Don't worry, we're here to help,"
said Fred and Big Max.

Fred and Big Max dived into the waves.
They went to the bottom of the sea.

"Look," said Fred, "there are the enemy robots."
"They are destroying the oil rig.
It's moving! Stop them."

Big Max and the enemy robot
had a fight at the bottom of the sea.
Fred was scared.

"Please win," he said.
"I don't want to be alone at the bottom of the sea."

Big Max and the enemy robot had a long fight.

Big Max was hurt, but he won the fight.
He put the oil rig back on
the bottom of the sea.

The men on the oil rig gave Fred and
Big Max a big breakfast.
They ate a lot.
On the news it said the oil rig was safe.